OUR ENVIRONMENT

STEWART ROSS

Wayland

Stewart Ross

STARTING HISTORY

Food We Ate
How We Travelled
Our Environment
Our Family
Our Health
Our Holidays
Our Schools
Shopping
What We Wore
Where We Lived

First published in 1992 by
Wayland (Publishers) Ltd
61 Western Road, Hove
East Sussex, BN3 1JD

© Copyright 1992 Wayland (Publishers) Ltd

Editor: Geraldine Purcell
Series Designer: Derek Lee

British Library Cataloguing in Publication Data

Ross, Stewart
Our Environment.—
(Starting History Series)
I. Title   II. Series
333.70941
ISBN 0-7502-0628-4

Typeset by Dorchester Typesetting Group Ltd
Printed and bound in Belgium by Casterman S.A.

PICTURE ACKNOWLEDGEMENTS
East Sussex County Library 9, 27; E.T.
Archives Ltd 13 (bottom), 25 (bottom); Eye
Ubiquitous (P Thomson) 14; Frank Lane
Agency 4, 8, 20; The Billie Love
Collection 6, 24; The Mansell Collection
16; Popperfoto Cover, 5, 15; Topham 7
(bottom), 12, 17 (bottom), 19 (bottom), 21
(bottom), 23, 28, 29 (bottom); Wayland
Picture Library (Zul Mukhida) 7 (top), 13
(top), 17 (top), 19 (top), 21 (top), 25 (top),
29 (top); West Sussex County Council
Library Service 10, 11; ZEFA 18, 22, 26.

Words that appear in **bold** are
explained in the glossary on
page 31.

Starting History is designed to be used
as a source material for Key Stage
One of the National History
Curriculum. The main text and
photographs reflect the requirements
of AT1 (Understanding history in its
context) and AT3 (Acquiring and
evaluating historical information).
The personal accounts are intended to
introduce different points of view
(AT2 – Understanding points of view
and interpretations), and suggestions
for activities and further research
(AT3 – Development of ability to
acquire evidence from historical
sources) can be found on page 31.

CONTENTS

THE CHANGING WORLD

This photograph was taken from an aeroplane. Can you see the roads, houses, gardens and fields?

Almost everything in this picture was made by people. We have been changing our **environment** for hundreds of years. Sometimes we make it better, but often we make it worse. This book will tell you how we have changed it.

Here is an **industrial** town in 1970. Can you see the dirty smoke coming from the **factory** chimneys? Do you think it was a good environment for a child to grow up in? Today the air looks much cleaner. Factories are not allowed to make too much smoke. In some ways the environment is better than it was then.

This is what much of our countryside looked like over one hundred years ago. Many people lived in small villages and towns. These were surrounded by farms and open spaces. The environment was not as **polluted** or damaged as it is today.

Ethel Good was born in 1937. She remembers how the environment has changed since she was a girl.

'When I was growing up the towns were very noisy and dirty, but the countryside around them was quiet and clean. There was lots of wildlife, and more trees and hedges than I see now. My sister and I knew the names of dozens of wild flowers.

'Of course, there is still some beautiful countryside left. But there seem to be factories, roads and houses everywhere. Pollution and **overcrowding** seem to be spoiling our environment.'

7

Look at all these houses! When lots of houses are built together like this, it is called a housing estate.

Today over 45 million more people live in Britain than 300 years ago. As the **population** grew, more and more homes had to be built for the extra people. Towns and cities spread into the countryside and farming areas. Are you surprised that the environment has changed so much?

This is the village of Alfriston in East Sussex, almost one hundred years ago. Only a few hundred people lived there then.

Now the population of Alfriston is over one thousand people. The village has changed completely. People have to live somewhere, so housing estates have been built over the old fields. Do you live in a village, town or city?

This is the high street in the large town of Crawley. Fifty years ago Crawley used to be a small village. After the **Second World War** many new shops and houses were built. Are there any new shops where you live?

New towns can be pleasant to live in, but the new buildings take up a lot of land that was once farms and open countryside.

Can you guess where this is? It is the high street in Crawley, in 1903. Crawley was still a village then.

Look at the two pictures carefully. What differences can you see? Some people think it is a shame to knock down old buildings. What do you think?

Can you see the two roads in this picture from 1936? The road with the horses on it is very old and narrow. The car is being driven along the new road.

Over the last two **centuries** railways and new roads have been built through the countryside. This has changed the environment a lot.

Tommy Wheeler remembers how a motorway has changed the **landscape** where he used to live.

'I'm the boy on the right in the field. We were picking peas in 1932. The only sounds were the birds singing and my mum saying that her back hurt.
    'There is a motorway covering that field now. You can't hear the birds because of the roar of the cars. It's a pity, but I suppose we need good roads these days.'

FRESH AIR?

These people are walking to work in the middle of London. Can you see the **traffic** in the background?

The air looks clean, doesn't it? In fact it is full of pollution from factories and car **exhaust fumes**. Even pollution that we cannot see can **poison** the air we breathe.

Look at the dirty smoke coming from these factory chimneys! The picture was taken in 1969. Factories used to produce lots of smoke, even if they were close to people's homes.

Laws were passed to stop this kind of pollution. Today factories are not allowed to make so much smoke. But some still pollute the air with dirt we cannot see. This pollution can still harm our health.

This is a drawing of a London street in 1905. It is daytime but all the street lights are on. London used to be famous for scenes like this. It shows how bad the air was earlier this century.

In those days most houses and factories had coal fires. The smoke from the fires mixed with fog to make poisonous smog. During a heavy smog it was difficult to see and some people found it hard to breathe.

Anne Blair lived in London in the 1950s. She remembers the terrible smogs very clearly.

'In November 1953 the smog was so thick we couldn't see the other side of the street. My husband and I made cloth masks to help us to breathe. We felt a bit silly, but at least the smog didn't get into our lungs.

'Nowadays I think I need another mask, to keep out the car exhaust pollution.'

WHAT A NOISE!

What is this boy doing? He is putting his fingers in his ears to keep out the noise of the aeroplane.

Noise pollution is very bad today. Wherever people live there are lots of cars and often noisy building sites. It is difficult to find a really quiet place. Which makes the most noise: aeroplanes, cars, lorries or motorbikes?

George Chambers remembers how quiet the countryside was before the Second World War.

'My wife took this picture in 1938. We stopped beside the road, switched off the car engine, and listened. There wasn't a sound except for a few tractors being used on a nearby farm.

'The other day we went back to the same spot. Someone was playing a radio, planes were flying overhead and the traffic noise was awful. I think noise pollution ruins our environment.'

19

DIRTY WATER

Would you like to play on this beach? It is covered with rubbish and other pollution which has been thrown into the sea.

For a long time we have used the sea as a rubbish dump. Now it is so polluted that in some places fish are dying, and it is not safe to swim.

John Milne is thirty-seven. When he was young he used to go fishing by the river near his home.

'I loved going fishing in the summer. My older brother used to take me to a safe place by the river. We had a great time and caught lots of fish. Nowadays many rivers are polluted by dirty water from farms and factories. You don't see so many fish in the rivers. I think this means they are dangerous for us too!'

ON THE FARM

Do you know what is going on here? It is **harvest** time on a modern farm.

Farms are like food factories. Most farmers need to grow crops in huge fields, with no hedges. They use lots of machinery, **fertilizers** and weed-killers to produce plenty of cheap food. Modern farming has changed our environment.

Can you see the farmer in this picture
taken in 1963? What is he doing?

At this time many farmers were
beginning to pull out hedges to make big
fields, and putting lots of fertilizers into the
ground. They did not know that they were
damaging the environment.

This man is cutting hay in 1914. His machine is pulled by two horses. Can you see the tall hedge at the side of the field? Do you see many hedges like this today?

In 1914 the countryside had not changed very much for two centuries. But after the Second World War new ways of farming began to change the countryside very fast.

Alf Martin was brought up on a farm before the Second World War.

'Do you like this picture? It's my dad **ploughing** with our horses, Daisy, Dan and Dru in 1938.
   'My dad loved the countryside and never wanted to harm it. He had never heard of *environment* or *pollution*. He just farmed the way his dad and grandad had done. But, he didn't produce half as much food as a modern farm.'

WILD PLACES

After the Second World War the countryside changed very quickly. Towns grew, new roads and motorways were built. Hedges and woodland were dug up. To keep beautiful places the way they were, **national parks** were set up. Everyone can go to these areas to enjoy the lovely countryside.

The tents in this picture are on a **camp site** in a national park in the Lake District. Have you ever slept in a tent?

This is what happens to our environment when builders are allowed to build anywhere they want. These new houses were built in the 1950s. Do you think they fit in with the landscape?

Forty years ago some people thought that there would soon be no countryside left. Do you think that we should still worry about this now?

This picture of the Lake District was taken in 1953. In those days not many people visited **remote** places in Britain. Far fewer people had cars. You could walk all day without seeing anyone else.

This has changed. Some national parks are being damaged by all the people going there. Have you been to a national park?

I REMEMBER . . .

Joe Cook used to go on holidays to the Lake District in the 1950s.

'My dad used to take us to the Lake District for our summer holidays. It was a long drive but the scenery was beautiful so we didn't mind.

'We spent all summer walking and horse riding through the countryside. It was great fun.

'I went back to the same place last summer. There were lots more people. Some of them were dropping rubbish all over the place. What a shame!'

Talking to people

Ask grown-ups you know well about the changes they remember in the environment. You could ask them about the countryside, the air, water and noise. What are the biggest changes they remember? Have things got better or worse? You could write down their answers in a scrapbook and illustrate them with drawings or old photographs and pictures from magazines.

Use your eyes

Another good way to find out about how the environment has changed is to look at the pictures in old books, papers and magazines. There may be a museum nearby where you can see how the place where you live has changed in the last hundred years.

Read all about it

These modern books are also useful:
The Green Detective series: (Wayland, 1991-1992)

Making a display

What about making a display of 'Our Environment' in your classroom? Try to show how things have changed over the last century. You could use what you have learnt from this book and from talking to grown-ups. Do not forget that the past was not better or worse than today, just different.

GLOSSARY

Camp site   A place where tents can be set up.

Centuries   Periods of one hundred years. We live in the twentieth century, which began in 1901. It will end in the year 2000.

Environment   Everything that is around us.

Exhaust fumes   The dirty air and gases that come from the engines of cars or lorries.

Factory   A large building where goods are made.

Fertilizers   Fertilizers are put on fields to help plants grow. They can harm humans if they get into our drinking water.

Harvest   When crops are brought in from the fields.

Industrial   An industrial town or area is one with a lot of factories in it.

Landscape   The look of the countryside.

National parks   Beautiful parts of the countryside where the landscape must not be changed.

Overcrowding   When too many people live in an area.

Ploughing Turning over the top layer of ground to loosen the soil.

Poison   To put harmful substances into the air.

Polluted   Harmed by poisons or dirt.

Population   The number of people living in a place.

Remote   Out of the way and difficult to get to.

Second World War   The war that lasted from 1939 to 1945.

Traffic   All the cars, lorries, vans and cycles moving on a road.

INDEX